DISASTROUS DEATHS

FRIGHTFUL FOOD

RIP

Written by
Mignonne
Gunasekara

Designed by
Jasmine Pointer

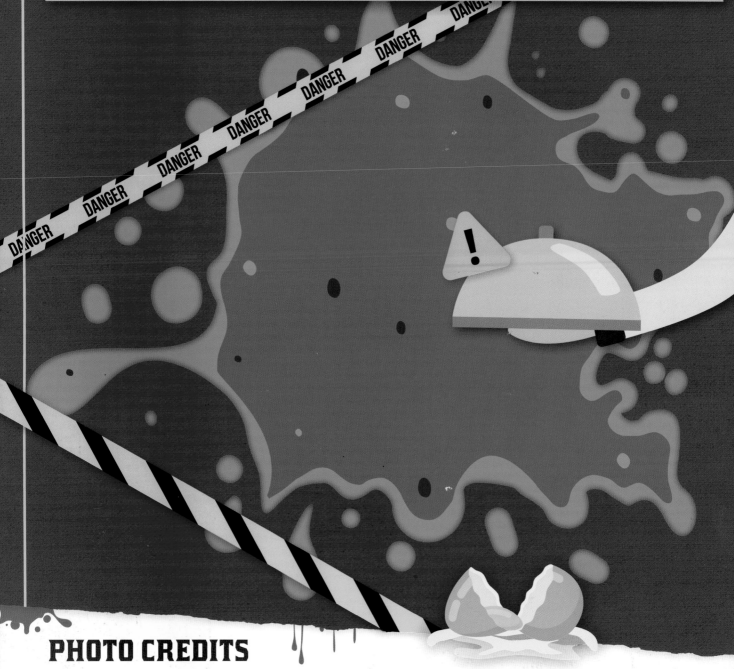

BookLife PUBLISHING

©2020
BookLife Publishing Ltd.
King's Lynn
Norfolk PE30 4LS

All rights reserved.
Printed in Malaysia.

A catalogue record for this book is available from the British Library.

ISBN: 978-1-83927-815-0

Written by:
Mignonne Gunasekara

Edited by:
John Wood

Designed by:
Jasmine Pointer

PHOTO CREDITS

All images are courtesy of Shutterstock.com, unless otherwise specified. With thanks to Getty Images, Thinkstock Photo and iStockphoto. Background texture throughout – Abstracto. Gravestone throughout – MaryValery. Front Cover – Viktorija Reuta, Inspiring, Anatolir. 4 – pashabo, Lilkin, PixMarket. 5 – Maquiladora, Rawpixel.com, IYIKON, Krasovski Dmitri. 6 – Elegant Solution, HappyPictures, HN Works. 7 – trabantos, RRA79. 8 – Gustaf Lundberg [Public domain]*, Everett Historical. 9 – Mauritshuis [CC0], Georgios Kollidas, Kunturtle, Tayka_ya, Tomacco. 11 – Ton Reijnaerdts, NotionPic. 12 – Germany [Public domain], ottoflick, Anatolir. 13 – PHOTO FUN, COULANGES, ONYXprj. 15 – Pinkyone. 16 – Everett Historical, Djvu created by me [Public domain], ONYXprj. 17 – Everett - Art, https://commons.wikimedia.org/wiki/File:Louis-Michel_van_Loo_001.jpg*. 18 – Boyko.Pictures, Orn Rin. 19 – GoodStudio, oticki. 20 – Everett Historical, oticki. 21 – akepong srichaichana, Tupungato, Roi and Roi, Pogorelova Olga. 22 – Lucia Fox. 23 – SofiaV, Osman Vector, Africa Studio. 24 – godrick, mejorana, Mila star. 25 – Volosina, William Hogarth [Public domain], Arisa_J. 26 – ONYXprj, MuchMania. 27 – Kevin5017. 28 – https://commons.wikimedia.org/wiki/File:Qinshihuang.jpg, Sofiaworld, MuchMania, hanukuro. 29 – lzf, Fedor Selivanov, LynxVector. *U.S. work public domain in the U.S. for unspecified reason but presumably because it was published in the U.S. before 1924. Additional illustrations by Jasmine Pointer.

CONTENTS

Words that look like <u>this</u> are explained in the glossary on page 31.

WELCOME
TO THE
DISASTER ZONE

History is full of grisly stories and weird tales... and a lot of death. From the battlefield to the home, from rich royals to those who didn't have much money at all, people in the past got up to some pretty strange stuff during their lives. So it makes perfect sense for some of those people's lives to have ended in ways that were just as strange.

Around seven percent of all the people who have ever lived are alive right now. How cool is that? You know what that means... there are loads of deaths to choose from!

In this book, we are going to look at the stories of several people who were taken out by frightful food and dreadful drink. Whether it was overeating, <u>contamination</u> or an extreme love of the simple bean, we'll find out about the many food-and drink-related ways in which these unfortunate people met their disastrous ends.

INTO THE DISASTER ZONE WE GO...

Throughout history, there have been lots of names and sayings that mean someone has died.

croak

Here are a few of the weird ones:

**Kicked the bucket
Bit the dust
Croaked
Six feet under
Popped their clogs
Pushing daisies**

ADOLF FREDERICK OF SWEDEN

The year was 1771. It was Shrove Tuesday, otherwise known as Fat Tuesday. Many people see Fat Tuesday as a day of eating fancy foods before giving them up for <u>Lent</u>, which starts the next day. And that was exactly what Adolf Frederick, King of Sweden, was doing.

He ate lobsters, caviar, sauerkraut and kippers, and washed it all down with champagne. And that was just for his main course. Adolf had his favourite sweet treat ready for dessert – semla, a type of cream-filled bun. He helped himself to 14 of these buns! Eating all this food was not good for Adolf, and he died of either food poisoning or <u>indigestion</u> very soon after this massive meal.

Adolf Frederick was mostly a <u>figurehead</u> as king, because he had very few powers. Sweden was <u>governed</u> by a <u>parliament</u>.

EAT YOUR LIFE OUT

Adolf Frederick is not the only royal to have enjoyed grand meals in the past. Queen Victoria always had a big appetite and loved to eat. After her husband died, she started to eat a lot more to comfort herself and this made her gain a lot of weight.

Adolf Frederick of Sweden

Some people say Queen Victoria could eat several courses of food in just 30 minutes.

During Henry VIII's time, royals would sometimes have a whole bird, such as a swan or peacock, served at dinner. It would have its skin with the feathers still in place removed before cooking and put back on after cooking. This made the birds look alive on the table.

These birds were <u>status symbols</u> because only the very wealthy could afford to pay for chefs to carefully prepare them.

Not cool.

A roast swan may have looked something like this.

Charles II was known for his love of dinner parties. He and his closest friends would sit on a raised table so that everyone else in the room could see them. Servers would offer them first pick of the food, and taste it to make sure it was safe.

Charles II was a king who ruled over England, Scotland and Ireland during the 17th century.

Charles II was a king of firsts. Rumour has it that he was one of the first people in England to try a pineapple. The first written mention of ice cream is on the menu for one of Charles' banquets.

MRS TROFFEA
AND THE
DANCING PLAGUE

Something extraordinary happened in Strasbourg in the summer of 1518. It started with one woman, named Mrs Troffea. She started to dance… and didn't stop. Within a week, she'd been joined by around 34 people, all dancing in the dark and daylight through Strasbourg's streets.

The city's leaders decided that everyone was ill with 'overheated blood' and the only cure was to let them dance until they felt better. They cleared spaces in the city for people to dance and hired musicians to play pipes and drums. They also hired professional dancers to dance with the ill people and keep them on their feet. But this made things worse, and people were starting to drop dead from all the dancing.

Some people say that around 15 dancers collapsed every day and died from things such as exhaustion, heart attacks and strokes.

Born: ???
Died: Strasbourg, France
Claim to fame: Knew how to party
Death by: Dancing
I'm going to dance until I drop!
DIED 1518

FEVER FOOD

The dancing plague started in mid-July and was over by September. At its worst, in August, around 400 people were caught up in it. The dancing only stopped when the city's leaders started taking the ill people to a <u>holy shrine</u>, where they were 'healed'.

YE OLDE FLASH MOB

People still don't really know why this happened. A popular idea was that people had eaten bread or other foods that were contaminated with ergot. Eating ergot can make people see things that aren't real.

Tired dancers were held up so they kept dancing.

Strasbourg

Strasbourg is not the only place to have had a dancing plague, but it was one of the last.

The ergot fungus growing on rye

Ergot poisoning would have also made the people ill in ways that make dancing difficult, so this is an unlikely explanation.

In It Together

The most likely explanation for the dancing plague is mass panic. This is when several people start acting in strange ways for no reason. Mass panic tends to happen in times of stress, and Strasbourg had a lot of disease and <u>famine</u> at the time. Another thing is that the people at the time believed in St Vitus, a religious figure who was supposed to be able to punish people by making them dance uncontrollably.

Ergot growing on corn

DENIS DIDEROT

Denis Diderot was a <u>philosopher</u> who wasn't afraid to question things. He even questioned religion, which was very important at the time, and he got into a lot of trouble with the Church and the government for it.

The story goes that even though he was such a clever person, Denis had a <u>guilty pleasure</u>. He loved to eat. One day, even though he was very sick, Denis ate a huge meal. As he reached for an apricot for dessert, he was told by his family that he'd probably eaten enough. "How the devil can that hurt me?" asked Denis. He ate the apricot... and ended up passing away soon after. Maybe he should have listened to his family.

Denis's father stopped giving him money when Denis decided to become a writer instead of a doctor or lawyer. How mean!

BORN: Langres, France
DIED: Paris, France
CLAIM TO FAME: Famous philosopher
DEATH BY: Apricot

TOLD YOU SO

Denis Diderot was an important writer and philosopher during the Enlightenment. This was a time of change where people looked to question the power and decisions of the people in charge, and use philosophy to improve the lives of everyone.

Denis Diderot

Denis's writing often questioned the Bible and the idea of religion – this made both the Catholic Church and the French government angry. They tried to stop Denis from getting his writing to his readers. When Denis kept writing anyway, they sent him to prison. Even this didn't stop Denis.

Philosophy is the study of life. It involves asking questions about how people should live their lives.

When Denis got out of prison, he began writing 'Encyclopédie', which would become his most famous project. This work caught the attention of many people around the world, including that of Empress Catherine the Great of Russia.

'Encyclopédie', one of Denis's writing projects

Catherine the Great was a big fan of Denis's work

Denis wrote everything from plays to novels. When people were upset with his books, they would burn them.

Thanks, Catherine! You really are great.

Catherine the Great liked Denis's work so much that she helped him out when he was running out of money. She bought his library, but said that Denis could keep all his books until he died. She also paid him a yearly salary to be her librarian. Denis never had to worry about money again.

PYTHAGORAS

Pythagoras was a Greek mathematician and philosopher. He had a lot of great ideas, which he taught to his students, the Pythagoreans. At some point, people began to dislike the power they thought Pythagoras and his students had. They didn't want Pythagoras to spread his ideas around anymore so they decided to shut him up for good.

The story goes that Pythagoras was being chased by an angry mob. He was doing a good job of running away – until he came upon a field of bean plants. Pythagoras thought beans were really important, so he didn't want to run across the field and trample them. Unfortunately, this gave the mob enough time to catch up with Pythagoras. He gave his life for those beans.

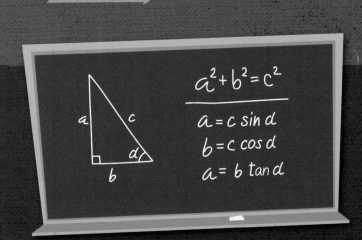

$$a^2 + b^2 = c^2$$

$a = c \sin d$

$b = c \cos d$

$a = b \tan d$

Some of the ideas that Pythagoras had about life, music and maths all those years ago are still important today.

HE MUST'VE BEAN JOKING

Why did Pythagoras care that much about boring old beans? We may never know for sure, because Pythagoras didn't like to write things down and his students had to all promise to keep what they talked about a secret.

Aside from never eating beans, Pythagoras and his students were all vegetarians and wouldn't wear animal skins or wool.

Pythagoras

A field of soybeans

What we do know tells us that the Pythagoreans lived their lives by following a strict set of rules. They believed that following these rules was the way to live a good life. The first rule was that maths is the meaning of life, and the second was NO BEANS.

WHAT DO YOU BEAN?

Some say Pythagoras believed that beans and humans were so similar that eating or damaging beans was like eating or hurting a human. The Pythagoreans believed in reincarnation. This is the belief that when you die, you will come back to start a new life in another body. The body could be of an animal, plant or human. Pythagoras believed that beans played an important part in reincarnation.

Other people say that the reason Pythagoras didn't eat beans was because he thought they distracted him from work. Beans are known to make people gassy – that's pretty distracting!

The Pythagoreans didn't eat animals in the hope that they could come back with a good body in the next life.

PITAGORA

A statue of Pythagoras

21

HENRY PURCELL

Many people think that Henry Purcell is one of Britain's greatest <u>composers</u>. He got a lot done by a young age – he composed music for Charles II, James II and William and Mary of Orange.

Nobody is sure how he died. Here are two of the ways people believed it may have happened. The first is that he got sick after staying out late with his friends. They had been to the theatre, but took their time getting home. It was a cold night and Henry ended up being locked out of his house. The second story is that he got food poisoning from some chocolate he drank at a cocoa house. These are cafés that just serve chocolate. They were the new exciting thing in London in 1695.

Henry probably actually died from tuberculosis, an illness that mainly affects the lungs. It had no cure during Henry's time.

OUT ON A LOW NOTE

Henry Purcell and the music he composed were very important in what is known as the Baroque period. This musical period lasted from around 1600 to 1750.

Henry Purcell

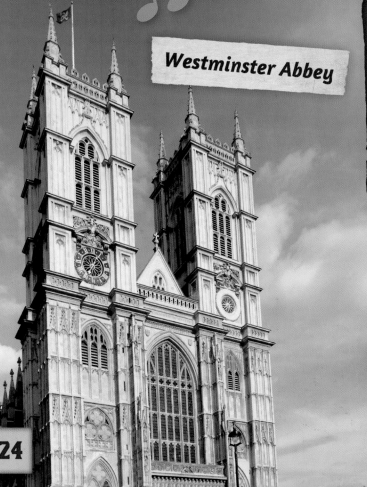

Westminster Abbey

Henry composed everything from church music to music for special occasions such as birthdays – even royal birthdays. He worked for kings and queens, and had even been selected to play the organ at Westminster Abbey by the time he was just 20 years old. Henry is now buried in the abbey, where the organ he played used to be.

A lot of people still love Henry's music, and a lot of musicians look up to him.

Hot chocolate was quite a different drink in the 17th century. It wasn't made with milk. Instead, flavours such as citrus, vanilla and jasmine or spices such as cinnamon and cloves were added to it. It was an expensive drink, so only people with a lot of money could buy it.

This is what people may have got up to in a chocolate house.

Chocolate houses were used as a place to drink chocolate... but also to gamble, and even plot against kings!

Cocoa houses, or chocolate houses, were not as cute as they sound. They were a place for people to spend time with each other, but sadly not everyone spent that time wisely. Things could get a bit messy.

QIN SHI HUANGDI

Qin Shi Huangdi was born as Ying Zheng, the son of King Zhuangxiang of Qin. He became the first emperor to rule over every part of China. Over the years, Qin Shi Huangdi became obsessed with living forever. He spent a lot of time and money on searching for a way to do so, or at least a way to make him live longer. He was willing to pay anyone who could solve this problem for him.

One person brought Qin Shi Huangdi a medicine that would make him live longer if he took it every day. The only problem was that it was made with mercury, which is harmful to humans. Qin Shi Huangdi was dead before he was 50 years old.

Qin Shi Huangdi chose his own name to celebrate his achievements as emperor. 'Shi Huang' means 'first emperor'.

LIVE FOREVER...
OR DON'T

CHANGE IT UP

When Qin Shi Huangdi became emperor, he made sure that everyone used the same money, the same way of measuring things, and the same way of writing. He made sure that everyone followed the same laws and he built lots of new roads and other important structures.

Qin Shi Huangdi

Qin Shi Huangdi wanted to defend China against attackers from the north, so he decided to join up several smaller walls to make one big, stronger wall that would be harder for an enemy to get past. This was the start of the Great Wall of China.

The Great Wall of China

Qin Shi Huangdi's wall was 5,000 kilometres long. The Great Wall of China is over 21,000 kilometres long today.

TERRACOTTA ARMY

Qin Shi Huangdi is famous for where he was buried. Throughout his life, he had around 700,000 workers build him a giant tomb that took up 50 square kilometres! To guard this tomb, he had the workers build an army of around 8,000 life-sized soldiers out of terracotta, a type of clay.

Qin Shi Huangdi's Terracotta Soldiers

Each soldier's face looks different and they are all arranged the way they would be in battle. The soldiers carried real weapons such as spears, swords and bows and arrows, to protect Qin Shi Huangdi after death.

A square kilometre is a square area where each side is a kilometre long.

The terracotta army even had hundreds of horses and hundreds of working chariots

TIMELINE OF DEATH

PYTHAGORAS

500 BC

→

QIN SHI HUANGDI

210 BC

→

MRS TROFFEA

1518

DENIS DIDEROT

1784

←

ADOLF FREDERICK OF SWEDEN

1771

←

HENRY PURCELL

1695

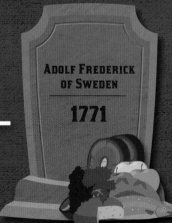

GLOSSARY

BC	meaning 'before Christ', it is used to mark dates that occurred before the starting year of most calendars
COMPOSERS	people who write music, especially as their job
CONTAMINATION	to make something unclean by adding a poisonous or polluting part to it
EXHAUSTION	to be very tired and have little energy
FAMINE	when large numbers of people do not have enough food
FIGUREHEAD	a leader without real power
GOVERNED	controlled or directed, especially politically
GUILTY PLEASURE	something a person enjoys even though it is not good
HOLY SHRINE	a place or thing dedicated to a religious figure, that people may worship at
INDIGESTION	a feeling of pain or discomfort in the stomach when there is trouble digesting food
LENT	a Christian religious period just before Easter, when people fast or give up things to show their love for Jesus
PARLIAMENT	a group of people who make the laws for a country
PHILOSOPHER	a person who studies the nature of knowledge, reality and existence
STATUS SYMBOLS	things that show how rich or important someone is

INDEX